D1644950

DRAWINGS FROM LIFE

DRAWINGS
FROM LIFE
by Eric Gill

London : Hague & Gill Ltd

Printed & made in Great Britain
by Hague Gill & Davey, High Wycombe
and Kimble & Bradford
for Hague & Gill Ltd
and published by them
at 10-12 Bedford Street, London W. C. 2
First published 1940

INTRODUCTION

Nakedness is the only nobility left to the vast majority of contemporary men: their clothes, far from being for dignity and adornment, degrade them. Apart from their vulgarity when new, how often does one not see a godlike torso emerging from filthy nth-rate garments, almost radiant with the visible touch of the Creator! If naked bodies can arouse a hell-hunger of lust, they can and do kindle a hunger for heaven. May God bring us all thither . . .

(from a letter of a Catholic priest)

In the business of 'drawing from the life' there seem to be two chief things to be considered—the thing seen, and the thing, the drawing, made, and both these things must be considered in all their causes. First then, what is the thing seen? Let us suppose that by 'the life' we mean the nude human body. It is clear at once that we are concerned with a thing both animal and human in its nature—a compound of matter and spirit, of the measurable and the immeasurable, and we must consider these two things separately, however inseparable they may be in the model. See postscript A.

Now an animal, though it be 'living', is not therefore in any way less subject to what we roughly and perhaps inaccurately call 'the laws of nature', and like all other material things it acts, behaves, 'carries on', apart from miraculous interference, according to the general 'rule' or statement that all material bodies follow the line of least resistance. This is the unchanging, unalterable, inexorable fact of nature. It makes no difference that the resistances seem to be both internal and external; nothing in nature either does or can behave otherwise. I do not wish, if only because it would be impossible for me to do so, to set the matter out in what we

i

call scientific terms. What I wish to point out, because I do not think it is commonly appreciated or insisted upon, is the simple fact that all those things which we call 'the beauties of nature', the most simple, and the most subtle and complicated, are not only nothing more than, but are precisely the product of the universal obedience, thus to write rhetorically, of all material things. There is, so to say, no rebellion in nature; no effort to go against the least opponent. Every force has its full effect. The internal forces, if we may so call them, which are the nature of particular things, expend themselves without stint, and the only restraint which they suffer, or enjoy if you prefer, is that which is imposed upon them by the similarly unstinted forces to which they are subjected. Hence, strange as it may seem to us who are the victims of 'the pathetic fallacy' in all its applications, the beauties of nature, hence the loveliness of the world we live in.

Perhaps a simple illustration will make the matter clear. Suppose an ordinary billiard table. Suppose, to start with, one billiard ball covered with such a chalky substance as to show a white line on the board wherever the ball rolls. Give the ball a good knock and observe the line of its track as it bounces first from one cushion and then another. Supposing, for the sake of argument, that the ball does not happen to run into a pocket, this line will, if the ball run long enough, become a complicated pattern of intersecting V's, so complicated that, eventually, the whole board will be covered like a closely woven cloth. Now imagine several similar balls set in motion in the same way, but from different starting points. Obviously the resulting line pattern will be exceedingly more complicated. Imagine further that the billiard board itself be oscillated from side to side and, at the same time from end to end. The balls will then start to roll in curved tracks, and if after a time the whole thing were stopped and the balls removed, there would be disclosed a complicated but rhythmical pattern or series of patterns. Now let us introduce a human observer. He also, at least as regards his material composition, is the product of a long series of similar forces and is therefore prone to respond to those things which, as it were, harmonize with his own pattern. He will therefore find the rhythmical arrangement of lines on the billiard board more or less pleasing or displeasing. If he finds it pleasing he will call it beautiful and, being a philosopher, he will say: 'Beautiful things are those which being seen please'.

This object lesson is of course on a plane of simplicity only observable among inanimate objects. It is none the less useful as describing the elements of the matter. For when we observe living creatures, whether vegetable or animal, we must always remember that such is the basis of their beauty and that our own similar make-up is the basis of our appreciation. The cause of beauty among flowers and animals is the same cause as that of the beauty of crystals; the only difference is the vastly greater complication of the motions or forces to which they are subject. But, being ourselves the product of more complicated forces than any other creature, we are all the better placed to appreciate and respond to all lesser complications and therefore to discover harmony and balance and unity and proportion in all natural things, especially those which, unlike the ball pattern, do not depend on mere symmetricality for their beauty.

This matter might be expounded at much greater length,

but for the purposes of this essay or preface what I have said will perhaps be enough to show the perspicacious reader what I mean. It seems only necessary to say further that it is essential that we should not suppose that there is anything derogatory in thus arguing that natural beauty is the product of the perfect obedience of material things to so apparently unheroic a rule as that of 'least resistance'. 'Freedom', as Lenin is reported to have said, 'is knowledge of necessity;' and this profound saying, though lacking the completeness of the Christian dictum: 'The service of God is perfect freedom', does, nevertheless, suggest the truth of the matter. For though inanimate matter cannot, except metaphorically, be said to have knowledge, and freedom is an abstraction only appreciable by spiritual beings, it is true that rebellion against what is necessary is not only futile but destructive of order and therefore of all good, and productive of chaos and therefore of all the slaveries.

With regard to the beauty of the human body the point is this: we have got to discard the romantic notion that the shapes of our limbs and of our organs or those of anything else in nature are the product of 'design' in the modern art-school sense of the word, as though one should say: 'I will make this thing this shape because I like this shape, or I will make this machine such that it will be nice to look at.' 'God saw that it was good'—yes, and we also may say the same, but it is not therefore shown that God did or that we should follow any other 'law' than that of necessity—though in God's creation the 'law' is of his own making.

But the theory that I here expound is not simply that the shapes of things are in accord with the functions the things

iv

perform. It goes further than that. Form and function act and react on one another and it is as true to say that we walk because we have a suitable apparatus for doing so, as that our legs have the shape they have because we use them for walking with.

All this argument applies unreservedly to the whole world of irrational animals, plants and inanimate things. But man is undoubtedly something more—a rational person, therefore having freewill, therefore responsible for his acts, for his acts of disobedience and therefore for his obedience also. He is responsible for hating and also for loving and these motions of the soul are necessarily reflected in his body. The wounds inflicted by his hates or by the consequence of his hates, the sweetness and tenderness of his loves are seen in his limbs. You cannot draw this human animal and disregard these facts. If you do so, the result is a dead thing and that is perhaps why the 'life' drawings made by students in those dens of falsity we call art-schools are almost invariably tedious; for the wretched student is only concerned with shapes and structures and is totally regardless of the fact that he is drawing persons. But still the same 'law of necessity' prevails. Because the human body is that of a person it is not therefore free from the 'law' which governs all material things. The wounds of hate and the stigmata of love are reflected upon material and the material responds accordingly—it is a material response. And the draughtsman also is a lover. That is why he does it. Ultimately there can be no other reason. And his love is many sided. He must love not only the thing seen but the thing made also. This brings us to the second of the chief things to be considered—the drawing itself.

I do not wish to discuss here the art of drawing in its technical aspect. I cannot profess to know more than very little about it and that little is more a matter of morals than of technique—the sort of thing one tells children. Don't be careless, don't scribble. Remember that you are making a real thing and not merely a picture of a thing—a real thing and not an illusion, something really on your paper and not something which produces the effect of being something somewhere else. Put it there on purpose and not by accident.

'Art imitates nature', as Aristotle said, but, as St. Thomas Aquinas added, 'by working as she works', in *sua operatione*. For the work of art is in its essence not a copy of something seen with the bodily eye, not something seen as a photographic camera sees, not merely an imitation of the light and shade and colour of visible things; it is in its essence a translation into material of something seen inwardly, in the imagination, a thing created first of all in the mind and then reproduced in material. For though in a purely physical sense of the word the imagination is nothing but a recording and storing apparatus, there is another sense of the word, the sense commonly implied when we speak as human beings and not as scientists. In this other sense the imagination is actually a creative power. No material thing is known to us but by means of our five or more bodily senses, but what comes out of our minds is not therefore merely a material reflection or reproduction. For having grasped a thing by means of our senses we then in a manner digest it, turn it over and over, re-make it and re-form it. However short this period of contemplation be, it cannot fail of its effect, and here again we see the baneful effect of the common art-school training, a training chiefly designed to enable the student to pass examinations; for the student is not expected to use his imagination; he is not asked to contemplate the model; he is only urged to train his eye to see correctly and his hand to transcribe accurately what he sees. He is not encouraged to be human. He is not encouraged to create. But in the normal world we do not look at things in order to measure them but to make them our own, to possess them and in a manner to marry them and thus make them fruitful. The resulting 'image' is in a real sense a creation. For it is something which would not and could not otherwise exist. It is not made out of nothing, but it is a new thing. It is the product of intelligence and will. It is the product of love. It is in this sense that we are made in God's image. For we are really creators. We do really make things which otherwise are non-existent. We create being where there was no being. For this indeed we were made—that we might collaborate with God in creating—that we might carry further his created world and carry it further in the direction of God Himself— that we might improve on nature by making things which are the product of love and not mere obedience. God Himself cannot make what we can make except in the sense that He made us in order that we should make things thus—that we should add to the material world things which are not only the product of His 'law' but also the product of our love and therefore of our love of Him—things which not only express His love of Himself but do so willingly and consciously, an echo of Himself and an echo self-returning.

But so much talk of love is embarrassing in these days. We have so much degraded love by romanticism—made it nothing but self-love—that it has become suspect, a vague and unreliable sentiment, an emotional state, or else we associate it exclusively with tumescence. I shall not apologize. Fallen things must be lifted, vague things made clear. And nothing is more in need of rehabilitation among intelligible objects than love. Love, essentially friendship. Not precluding desire, nor even transcending it, but controlling its merely self-regarding components so that we desire even more passionately, not in order to possess but for the sake of what is beloved, and that is to say for God's sake. Love, essentially friendship; for among human beings the union of bodies is not the purely animal and instinctive reaction that many moralists seem to think, but is, even at its lowest and most careless, accompanied by and expressive of the union of minds. Love, essentially friendship. So that we are of one mind with what we love.

A drawing, then, is in its proper nature a work of creation and it is a thing created in a real collaboration with God. The artist, though without the need of wordy accompaniment, is like a pupil with his master, a master who, so to say, has 'left him to it'. I cannot help it if all this sounds impossibly pietistic. It is the plain truth. It is only necessary to say these things because four centuries of romanticism and secularization have driven them from our minds. God be praised if we can forget about it again and act as His friends without need of a reminder.

But here and now we must call ourselves back to the road. And even as all sin is in some way a sin against our neighbour so love of our neighbour is in some way implied in all that is not sinful. A drawing from 'the life' is therefore no more

to be thought of as an object of pure adoration of the beautiful than it is to be thought of as a more or less accurate
versimilitude or facsimile. It is neither that low thing—a
mere object of pleasure; nor is it that unwarrantably high
thing—a flattery of the Most High. We serve God by serving
our neighbours and if, by drawings, our neighbours are not
served, if, as we say, there is no place for such things—no
reasonable place, no place in a reasonable society—then they
have no reason for being; and they can have no proper place
if they do not serve at all or only serve our wantonness.

It is of course obvious that drawing from the life has its
usefulness as a means to the end of making useful images—
paintings or sculptures which, for one good reason or another,
serve our rational needs as citizens and pilgrims. But the
more important question here is: what possible place have
such drawings in themselves? In this difficulty I think we
have to argue quite frankly from the mere fact of our liking
for such things. 'We know in whom we believe' and we
know that the liking for such drawings is by no means con-
fined to those who do them. They are not merely studio
essays beloved of those who inhabit or frequent studios.
From the highest highbrow to the lowest hanger-on of high
finance—everyone delights, more or less, in pictures of
things—and, if they are honest with themselves, more rather
than less in pictures of the human body. They simply do so.
And so they buy photographs in rather shady shops, or they
buy drawings by Leonardo. Pornography as such and by the
very meaning of the word is an incitement to irregular, that
is to say irreligious behaviour. But not all drawings or photographs of the nude either are or are intended pornographic-

ally, nor are they always bought as such. Our love of such drawings is neither of necessity sinful nor the occasion of sin. Men and women under vows of celibacy are commonly shy of such works and, though there are many exceptions (and there has never been any formal Christian condemnation of nakedness, as such, or of its representation), we can appreciate their shyness. But for ordinary men and women 'in the world' there is reason for prudence but no reason for prudery and every reason against it. What then is the proper place for such drawings?

It seems impossible to escape the conclusion that as with all pictures, so with 'nudes' no less than with other figure paintings, landscapes or 'still life', the only proper description or definition of a picture is that it is a kind of ikon—a holy image. In more primitive times and places and, we are willing to admit it, in times and places more subject to ecclesiastical rule and influence, ikons almost invariably took the form of pictures of the Saints or of Christ and His Mother. These things have disappeared owing to the general secularization of life, but other pictures are still a kind of ikon and, in spite of everything, do still, both for painters and buyers, represent what is held to be good and, though it is not openly stated, holy. They represent a kind of worship, however little the fact be realized or admitted. And though it is infinitely regrettable that the old type of ikon is now rare and that most painters never paint such things (but that is not entirely their fault—for painters only get bread and butter by selling what people will buy and people today don't want 'holy pictures'—except penny prints to put in prayer books . . .) nevertheless we must not suppose that other kinds of pictures are not holy and that to represent what is holy is not their real reason for existence.

And then it must also be remembered that a certain good has come out of the evil. For though there ought normally to be a demand for ikons in the old sense, the great enthusiasm of the last four hundred years for pictures of 'nature'—landscapes, 'still life' and portraits and 'figure' subjects—has had the effect of greatly deepening our respect and admiration and love for the 'natural' world, the world which God created—its infinite beauty and subtlety, its grandeur and its solemnity, its sweetness and its terrors, even its comicality and, so to say, its Rabelaisian buffoonery and pig-stye coarseness. All these things are good and holy, and I don't see how it can be denied that we are today much more aware of these holinesses than would have been the case had we not been through the turmoils and corruptions of the post-Renaissance centuries.

We may thus see the kind of place drawings of the naked human body may and must have in our life. 'If naked bodies can arouse a hell-hunger of lust, they can and do kindle a hunger for Heaven.' That is the point. It is not merely that the artist is an interpreter of nature—one who sees more than others see, one who probes the shapes of things to discover the eternal types in the divine mind—though that is one of the functions of draughtsmanship and of the pictorial arts; it is rather that by pencil or paint the artist creates new and living images of God. There is not necessarily any untruth in saying that a painting of grass may as clearly represent something of God and as godly as a painting of St. Francis or one of the Crucifixion. The taboo placed upon the representation of the human figure in the Jewish law and in the law of Mahomet was not, I opine (and I am supported by learned authority), due to any prudery or Manichean dualism, but simply to the obvious fact that men are prone to idolatry and forgetfulness and are constantly liable to seduction. We forget the divine image and see only the lovely dimples; we forget the mother of God and see only a 'glamour girl'. Much more—it is obvious—in pictures of nakedness, we are liable to forget Agape and see only Eros. It is a frightful risk. Who can blame the prudent pastor if he forbid such things? Has it not always been man's temptation, 'to sign the pledge', to take vows of chastity or vegetarianism, to cut his cheek to spite his face? The whole history of man is a record of his reactions—his pendulum-swingings from extreme to extreme—a panic of prudence damming a flood of wantonness. It is not only Christian ministers who succumb to these panics. All men are the same. The puritanism of the nineteenth century is only the nineteenth century version of what many other centuries have produced.

But, to reverse the picture, who should blame the ardent draughtsman if he rebel against such taboos? No one denies the existence of pornography; but why be so uncharitable as to suppose that all nakedness, whether in the flesh or in pictures, is pornographic? On the other hand, heaven forbid that I should seem to preach an erotic mysticism. We know what we have seen and touched, both with the body and with the mind—and that these things are inseparable; for it is the man, the whole man, body and soul, who enjoys and not his eye or his hand merely or his mind alone—we know the unnerving loveliness, heart-breaking, tear-bringing, which sometimes, however rarely, shakes the soul of the man and of the draughtsman. We know the sense of contact with God Himself which such moments seem to bring—as though a sort of arrow pierced our heart. We know the pang of thankfulness which then overwhelms the mind. But I argue nothing from this; I am not so imprudent, nor so forgetful of the rails on which, of necessity, our human life, bread and butter-winning, home-building, road-making, shop-keeping, must run. I only know that the goodness of God is visible and tangible in all his works and that we may indeed taste and see how gracious the Lord is. And I know that we can in some sort share our visions with our fellow-men.

I say it is the whole man who enjoys, but we need not assume that he enjoys himself—that is simply himself that he is enjoying. That is one of the main troubles of today: we assume that enjoyment has a purely self-worshipping connotation. I enjoy an apple: but who and what am I? Does my enjoyment necessarily mean that the apple ministers to me? Or can it mean a ministry to God? All creation is a manifestation of God's love of Himself, and the truth is that we, His creatures, take a conscious part in that act of loving—it is not ourselves that we enjoy but Him.

In a good society, such as one can imagine, and such as in past times has sometimes been approached, there is no such phrase as 'enjoy myself'. That would be and was regarded as a sort of self-abuse. They talked about enjoying their wives or the theatre or their food, but never of enjoying themselves. And theology supported and confirmed this frame of mind. Dominum Deum tuum adorabis et illi soli servies.

These are presumptuous words with which to preface a

book of reproductions. I do not suggest that the pictures illustrate the text, I only hope that, in a manner, the text may illustrate the pictures.

POSTSCRIPT

(A) Though clothes are primarily for dignity and adornment and only secondarily for protection from the weather, modesty and convenience (i.e. things with pockets in them), it is a mistake to suppose that the human skin is not itself a form of clothes; for the skeleton and the 'bag of tricks' which we call the vital organs and the muscular apparatus are enclosed by skin, and that skin is a sort of intimate inner garment or underclothes. 'Drawings from life', therefore, should not be regarded as drawings of something naked. There is nothing really naked about a man without artificial clothes, unless he be flayed.

(B) Some say that hair on the body is meant for a veil, and it is curious therefore that it should be held indecent to draw it. Perhaps this convention is now weakening, and from my point of view it seems best to draw whatever is natural and normal and to trust to the good sense of people to see things in a reasonable manner.

(C) One of the difficulties of drawing from professional models is that, as a result of art-school conventions, they think some attitudes are 'nice' and some not. While I hope that none of the drawings here reproduced will give offence in this way, I hope that they will not be judged simply by what might be called *boudoir* standards.

As a sort of proof that none of the drawings here reproduced is to be taken as a 'likeness', it should be pointed out that they are all from the same girl friend.

(D) With reference to those parts of the human body which, because of their intimate conjunction with organs of drainage, suffer an opprobrium both unwarranted and psychologically dangerous, I think much trouble and misunderstanding can be avoided if we observe the world of flowers. Exactly as 'Roses and lilies fair on a lawn' display the sexual parts of the rose and the lily, so, in literal fact, our sexual parts are our flowers, and that is a decent and salutary and sweetening way in which to regard them. Vegetables cannot pursue their mates so they must needs proclaim their lusts. Human beings, like other animals, are gifted with the power of movement, so have not the same need of advertisement; moreover we have also other fish to fry. Reason and Prudence are needed to curb our appetites, but that does not alter the fact above mentioned. Prudence is necessary but not error, and nursery prejudices should not cloud our reason.

The drawings from which the reproductions in this book were made are about twice as big as the reproductions and therefore it has been impossible in many cases to reproduce much of the finer pencil lines & 'shading'. The reader's indulgence is asked.

DRAWINGS FROM LIFE

I

4

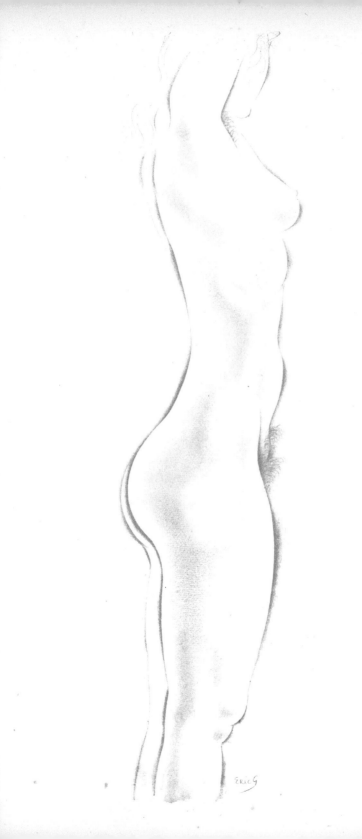

13

17

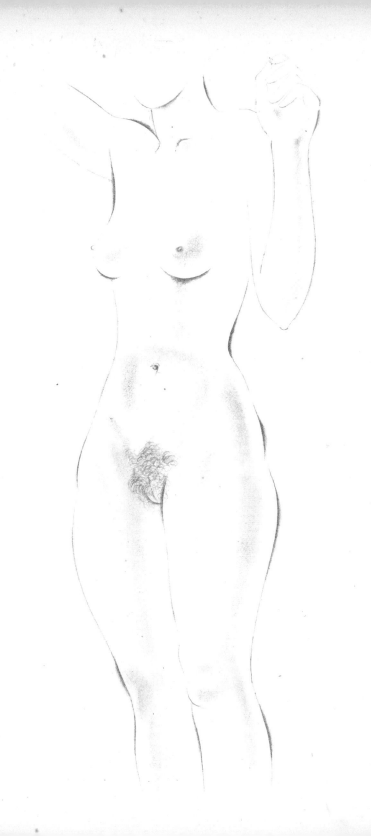